D1546866

A String Untouched

Dag Hammarskjöld's life
in haiku and photographs

Kai Falkman

Contents

Foreword   5

Prologue   7

Dag Hammarskjöld's life   9

The Photographer   13

The Haiku Poet   17

Haiku and Photographs   27

Epilogue   155

FOREWORD

This book is a translation from the Swedish original *En orörd sträng* (Ordfront, 2005). It contains a selection of 50 haiku poems from Dag Hammarskjöld's 110 haiku published in his posthumous work *Vägmärken* (1963, published in English 1964 as *Markings*). Two poems from the Swedish version have been omitted and two added.

The poems are reproduced in Swedish next to the English translation so that the reader can compare the texts and count the 17 syllables of the original Swedish haiku. In English no attempt has been made to count syllables.

The translations of Hammarskjöld's texts are made by the author of this book in order to render a text as close as possible to the Swedish original. In front of me I have had two old translations, W. H. Auden's *Markings* and Bernard Erling's *Waymarks* (1982). The translations by Erling are mostly closer to the Swedish text than Auden's—although sometimes less poetical—but both translations are faulty in certain respects and in Auden's case even contain guesswork and deliberate misconstructions.

Kim Loughran, English-speaking translator, has read through my manuscript and corrected some prepositions and Swenglish misnomers.

Kai Falkman

PROLOGUE

In the autumn of 1959 Dag Hammarskjöld wrote 110 haiku poems which were included in the manuscript of *Vägmärken* *(*Waymarks*)*, his private diary, published 1963, two years after his death. His fascination for the form of the Japanese short poem has been described as one of the greatest surprises in *Vägmärken*. These poems have been mentioned in several books about Hammarskjöld but have never been presented and analyzed as an independent literary genre. Here a selection of 50 poems has been made with commentaries that describe them from two perspectives: Hammarskjöld's and that of haiku poetry.

Dag Hammarskjöld was also a dedicated photographer. Wherever he went he always brought his camera along and even in the busiest of periods tried to find a way to practice his hobby. He enlarged his best photos and put them in albums, one photograph to a page. His 17 photo albums are, together with the manuscript of *Vägmärken* and letters, kept in the Dag Hammarskjöld collection at the Royal Library in Stockholm.

For this book I have selected 41 photographs, whereof 7 from a private collection of former Swedish ambassador Eric Virgin, who received two albums as a wedding gift from Hammarskjöld with photographs from sightseeing tours with Virgin´s car in France after the war when Virgin was Hammarskjöld's secretary at the Marshall Plan negotiations in Paris. The photos have been selected not as illustrations to the haiku but as independent complements. Even if several photographs depict the same motifs as in the haiku images, they are independent artistic expressions which present a play of lines, the distribution of light, the balance between detail and the whole. They show a pictorial perception which to a great extent corresponds with the image language of the haiku.

(* *Vägmärken* = *Waymarks*, from Jeremiah 31:21. "Set thee up waymarks...")

DAG HAMMARSKJÖLD'S LIFE

Dag Hammarskjöld was born on 29 July 1905 in Jönköping, Sweden. His father was Hjalmar Hammarskjöld, county governor of Uppsala 1907, prime minister 1914-1917, again county governor of Uppsala 1930. His mother was Agnes Hammarskjöld, née Almquist.

From generations of military men and civil servants on his father's side, "I inherited a belief", Dag Hammarskjöld says*, "that no life was more satisfactory than one of selfless service to your country—or humanity."

From generations of scholars and priests on his mother's side, he "inherited a belief that in the truly radical meaning of the gospels all men are equal as God's children, and should be met and treated by us as our masters in God." (*From Edward R. Murrow's radio programme "This I believe" in 1953)

Hammarskjöld grew up in Uppsala, studied French, economics and law at the University and received a Ph.D. in economics at Stockholm. At the age of thirty he became Under-Secretary of the Ministry of Finance and served concurrently as chairman of the Governors of the Bank of Sweden.

In 1947 he became Under-Secretary in the Ministry for Foreign Affairs in charge of all economic questions, and in 1949, when forty-four, he was appointed State Secretary for Foreign Affairs. Two years later he became a Minister in the Swedish Cabinet, regarding himself as a non-political civil servant without party affiliation.

As State Secretary and Minister he represented Sweden in the formative period of the Organization for European Economic Cooperation in Paris and the Council of Europe. He also represented his country at meetings of the General Assembly of the United Nations in New York. He spoke English, French and German with complete fluency.

Hammarskjöld's diplomatic skill at the Paris negotiations attracted the attention of French and British diplomats, who in the spring of 1953 suggested his name as Secretary-General of the UN after a search for candidates ended in deadlock. In April 1953, at the age of forty-seven, he was elected Secretary-General. The election was made against the background of the cold war between East and West and the wish of the great powers to find an non-political civil servant from a neutral country. Hammarskjöld soon emerged as a statesman and gave the United Nations a leading role in world politics.

His first prominent international breakthrough came in January 1955 when he went to Peking to negotiate with Communist China's leaders for the liberation of eleven American pilots shot down during the Korean war and imprisoned in China. After their release six months later, "the Peking formula" and "quiet diplomacy" became new diplomatic catchphrases attached to Hammarskjöld's name.

In 1956 he stood up against the British and French invasion of Egypt in the Suez crisis and organized the first UN peacekeeping troops to replace the invading troops. UN troops were also sent to the Congo in 1960 to restore peace and order after a breakdown of the newly independent state and to forestall involvement of the cold war parties in the African conflict. Hammarskjöld was asked to resign from his office by the Soviet Union but refused in the interest of all the other member states who needed the UN.

On a peace mission to reconcile the conflicting parties in the Congo Hammarskjöld died in a plane crash at Ndola just after midnight 18 September 1961.

Hammarskjöld was awarded the 1961 Nobel Peace Prize posthumously. His manuscript for *Vägmärken,* found in his bedroom in New York, he had described as "a kind of diary" with entries providing "the only true 'profile' that can be drawn." These entries, around 600, contain short sentences of severe self-examination and deep soul-searching based on moral, aesthetic and spiritual subjects. The haiku poems comprise more than one sixth of the entries. Also other kinds of verses occur, especially during his later years.

The texts in *Vägmärken* reflect Dag Hammarskjöld's wide literary and artistic interests with references to great authors of world literature, among them the medieval mystics. He himself worked on difficult literary translations from English (Djuna Barnes), French (Saint-John Perse) and German (Martin Buber). He was elected to succeed his father as a member of the Swedish Academy in 1954.

"The camera taught me to see", Hammarskjöld wrote in an article in the Swedish magazine Tidningen Foto, 1958. This was the most meaningful result of his perennially active interest in photography.

He concludes that it is better to learn to see than to have one's view decided by others: "However inferior our own products may seem compared to what others achieve, in the final analysis we learn more from our own than any number of pictures by the true artists of the camera, however great our debt of gratitude for their guidance."

The magazine had asked Hammarskjöld to present his 'best picture', which made him leaf through some older pictures. It became clear to him that there was none among them he could call a 'best picture', or even a really good one. "Too many criteria compete for the expression to have much meaning."

He comments on some pictures that he was attached to, for instance an evening scene of a thundercloud over the plain around Chartres (p. 58). "Technically it is questionable," he writes, "and yet the photograph is 'real', because it shows the play of forces around the cathedral which, its massiveness in human measurement notwithstanding, diminishes to a minor detail in the shadow of the cloud." The dark profile of the plain and the cathedral stand out sharply against a streak of light below the dominating black cloud.

Another picture he mentions is from a journey in Southeast Asia showing a poor Burmese woman at prayer before a reclining Buddha while her daughter impatiently follows the photographer's work (p. 88). It is a most vivid picture with the mother's back and the child's face illuminated by sunlight, while the large face of the Buddha smiles in the dusky background.

Hammarskjöld's Buddha pictures with their light and shadows and suggestive tones stand out as the most fascinating of the photo collection. They indicate an artist's eye that aims at rendering atmospheres beyond the play of forms.

Many photographs show the Swedish mountain world, among others a picture of the path along Abiskojokk (p. 78), "perhaps divulging its message only to the observer for whom the characteristic play of light over the landscape reflects a personal experience of such a timeless world at rest."

The white patches of snow in the landscapes and the foam of the waves reflect in some pictures patches of clouds in the sky so that ground, sea and sky flow together without boundaries.

The pictures reveal an eye open to barren trees and defoliated branches with "a play of lines reflecting the balance between power and nervous sensibility so often evidenced in nature's own creations." A photograph shows a withered stem with a barren crown that towers like a prehistoric lizard above the dry landscape (p. 44). These pictures recall the Japanese predilection for seasonal transitions when nature changes its colours.

In another sense too Hammarskjöld's motifs recall Japanese pictures: When the photos exceptionally show human beings, they emerge as temporary elements in the landscape, for instance the mountaineer (p. 129) or the man in the rowing-boat (p. 86). It is easy to recognize these as similar to the figures in Japanese Indian ink paintings of solitary fishermen as a point in a boat or under a tree on the shore. Landscape does not function as a background to human beings but as a central motif.

In the photographs, close-ups and wide views are depicted with the same sharpness. The backgrounds do not disappear in a haze behind the foreground motif; Hammarskjöld created drama through contrasting effects.

In the light between two dark cliff walls stand six Greek pillars as a human challenge to the primitive forces of nature (p. 74). Pillars erected to gods in a narrow opening of possibilities.

Five white flowers in a quiet dark pond, protected against the large sea behind firm rocks (p. 124). An arresting image of contrasts and likenesses.

Cartwheels in the sand, half buried, testify to a time long ago when the wheels were rolling on firm ground (p. 84). A symbol of the wheel of time, captured in a moment when the wanderer has stopped and turned the camera's eye of rebirth to the remains of human travail.

The frail shadow of a fragile tree across the sand of a beach shows a play of lines that gives strength of patience to the exposed situation. This tree constitutes a symbol of what Hammarskjöld calls "ultimate nakedness."

In Hammarskjöld's photographs there is a sense of "humility faced with the flower at the tree line which opens up the road to the mountain." He cautions against the temptation to appropriate, to swallow the experience of beauty, to pick the flower instead of "seeing" it as an expression of nature's inherent soul, inaccessible to physical touch. By taking a photograph of the flower he will be participating in the experience of beauty in two ways, first at the sight of the flower and the decision to photograph it, then at the revival after the development, when it has been transformed into a memory.

Still, Hammarskjöld asks himself what is the photographic value of his pictures? He does not deny the satisfaction of reaching a kind of self-fulfilment, both technical and aesthetic, in taking pictures, but he is aware of the risk of empty aestheticism if the picture is not marked by a spiritual experience of the senses.

On 4 August 1959 Dag Hammarskjöld made the following entry in *Vägmärken*:

> *Sjutton stavelser*
> *öppnade dörren*
> *för minnet och dess mening.*

> Seventeen syllables
> opened the door
> to memory and its meaning.

These three lines constitute a description of haiku, the Japanese short poem, which Hammarskjöld never mentions by name. They introduce the 110 haiku poems that he wrote between August and November 1959.

The poems are grouped under four headings: "From Uppsala, Summers, Far away, Hudson Valley." The first group of haiku poems comprises memories from his childhood in Uppsala, the second group from summers in Sweden, the third group from journeys far away and the last group from the Secretary-General's retreat (Brewster) in the Hudson Valley outside New York. Most of the poems are written from Hudson Valley (46) and from Uppsala (40), while the smallest number originates from far away journeys (8) and from Swedish summers (16).

-Why was it that precisely the haiku form opened the door to Hammarskjöld's memory? In the summer of 1959 he spent some time in Sweden for holidays, also visiting Uppsala. There, pictures from his youth must have reappeared, enticing him to find words for them. Why not in another kind of poetry or in short essays, like the one he wrote in the summer of 1961, "Castle Hill"?

Haiku was not well known in Sweden in the 1950s, but in the United States, Japanese Zen Buddhism and haiku had started to attract attention as a consequence of the American presence in Japan after the war. On Hammarskjöld's bedside table, Harold G. Henderson's book *An Introduction to Haiku* was found after his death. It was published in 1958 as an anthology with commentary of Japanese haiku poets from Basho (1644-1694) to Shiki (1866-1902).

Considering Hammarskjöld's intellectual and literary curiosity, it seems natural that he got to know haiku, especially as the admired poets of his youth, such as Ezra Pound and Paul Éluard had experimented with the haiku form in the beginning of the century.

Hammarskjöld's interest in Asian art and philosophy after his journeys to Asia in the 1950s was well known and probably also influenced his interest in haiku, even if he never travelled to Japan except for a short stopover in Tokyo on his journey from Laos in November 1959.

As difficult as it is to define a "best picture", it is just as difficult to define haiku, because haiku is so rich in expression and so variable in content. Basically haiku is a short poem which depicts a specific experience in nature or in human context that has impressed the poet. With as few and as exact words as possible the experience is described in a concrete image which aims at evoking the same view and feeling in the reader. A good haiku is not static but shows a transformation, if possible with a surprising ending or a lingering poetical atmosphere. This is the kernel of haiku, which has spread all over the world in the last half century and is now written in some 70 languages.

At the end of the 1950s haiku started to be written in Swedish by the poet Bo Setterlind and by Dag Hammarskjöld (his haiku unknown until 1963). They represent two different poetical forms: Setterlind used free form while Hammarskjöld followed the traditional Japanese rules of 17 syllables. These rules generally prescribe the grouping of syllables in the order of 5-7-5, but Hammarskjöld disregarded this order and grouped syllables differently from poem to poem. However, he always used three lines. He found the choice of words and rhythms more important than the counting of syllables, but still several of his poems have been burdened by superfluous words in order to fill the requirement of 17 syllables. It is interesting to note that contemporary

Swedish haiku poets are more or less evenly divided between upholders of 17 syllables grouped 5-7-5 and upholders of free verse, yet seldom exceeding 17 syllables.

The short and precise language of haiku must have appealed to Hammarskjöld, whose own literary style was pure and concentrated. An example from a poem written 1951, eight years before the haiku poems, testifies to a language that corresponds with haiku:

> *Knapp kost, fast form.*
> *Kort lust, få ord.*
> *En låg stjärna*
> *i sval rymd—*
> *en morgonstjärna.*

> Lean fare, solid form.
> Brief lust, few words.
> A low star
> in cool space—
> a morning star.

Hammarskjöld starts *Vägmärken* with a quotation attributed to the Swedish poet Bertil Malmberg: "Only the hand that erases can write the right thing." To find the right words in three lines to express an experience involves a careful examination of the values of the words and their combinations for maximal effect.

Most people who have read *Vägmärken* have paid little or no attention to the fact that the 110 poems from 1959 are haiku but have passed over them as a momentary departure from the prose text. In reality one third of the pages in the book comprise poetry, mainly haiku poems. They are the result of strict and time-consuming work with language and rhythms.

Half of the 110 poems depict clear and concrete images, as true haiku prescribes, while one third are abstract and the rest a mixture of concrete and abstract poems. The most concrete images are the ones which render childhood memories from Uppsala, while the largest part of the abstract poems are found under the heading "Hudson Valley", where Hammarskjöld spent week-ends and had time to think over matters that deeply concerned him. Recurring subjects among those are the choice between pleasure and duty, life and sacrifice, goodness and evil, to create or to destroy.

Purely intellectual poems cannot be characterized as proper haiku, because they cannot be made clear in concrete images. If form but not content is adapted to haiku, such poems may be described as poems using haiku format without being true haiku. Also belonging to this category are mixed poems with a concrete image that ends with an abstract idea—or vice versa. This type is found in 35 of Hammarskjöld's haiku and is much favoured among Swedish haiku poets.

Japanese readers are often confused by this kind of haiku. Even if they agree with the wise conclusion of the poem, the find it hard to accept its place in a haiku. Their view is that the image should be visually concrete so that it gives rise to the intended thought without any need to express it. A good haiku has a material quality inherently capable of producing several layers of meaning. If a meaningful insight, philosophical or spiritual, is directly expressed in the text, it may be interpreted as self-conceit or an imposition, which repels the reader. Poems of such content should rather be described as epigrams or aphorisms, and can be appreciated as such.

Japanese haiku principally describe nature, which must have appealed to Hammarskjöld, who often wrote and spoke about his love of Swedish nature. Most of his haiku are expressive descriptions of nature, which surprise the reader with their richness of names of trees, insects and herbs, often unusual ones such as *nattglim* (night-flowering catchfly), *kråkris* (crowberry), *isranunkel* (glacier crowfoot) and others difficult to find in a dictionary.

Hammarskjöld's 17 syllables opened the door to memory and its meaning. This indicates that in haiku his memories discovered a suitable form of expression. By using haiku he could be discreet and keep his distance, which also agrees with the spirit of haiku.

Several poems are mysterious and cryptic. They demand explanations and interpretations. In this book I have tried give the necessary background, departing from two perspectives: Hammarskjöld's own and the perspective of haiku.

The first is, of course, limited and relative, as I know Hammarskjöld only from his speeches, statements, texts and descriptions by his friends. The second perspective is more reliable after 40 years of haiku experience.

When *Vägmärken* was published in 1963, I had served for two years as attaché to the Swedish Embassy in Tokyo and had become interested in haiku, which I had read in Japanese and English (R.H. Blyth's volumes). Thus, Hammarskjöld's haiku in Swedish were a surprising experience. Now and then throughout the years I have returned to them, but while working with this book I discovered several haiku which my eyes had earlier passed over without discovering any deeper purport. Many haiku together on a page tend to compete with each other, so commentaries between the poems may be useful to give the reader occasion to pause and examine the content.

Haibun is the Japanese name for a mixture of haiku and prose, originally a travel story with poems. Later on the poems were quoted as independent haiku. Hammarskjöld's first four haiku under the heading "Far away" (pages 90-109) became easier to understand when I had read his travel story from Nepal in his essay "A New Look at Everest" in *National Geographic Magazine*.

Fundamentally, Hammarskjöld's haiku poems constitute a long travel story from his life as a young boy in Uppsala until his meeting with "the last miracle" in death. The 110 memory images form an autobiography in miniature of a kind hitherto unknown in Swedish literature. In this respect as in many others Dag Hammarskjöld was a pioneer.

His choice of haiku for the story of his life was logical: a haiku is a memorandum. Whenever a haiku is composed, immediately after the experience when feeling is most intense and memory most visual, or several decades later as in Hammarskjöld's case, the haiku is always a description of something that has happened in the past, be it immediate or long ago. But in the moment of the poem, the essence of the experience is revived and usually rendered in the present tense in order to communicate the feeling of here and now.

On the same day as Hammarskjöld wrote his first entry on Seventeen syllables, 4 August 1959, he made another reflection which heralds the haiku poems with a content that could serve as a philosophical principle for all haiku: "Simplicity is to experience reality not in relation to ourselves but in its holy independence. Simplicity is to see, judge and act from a point in which we rest in ourselves. /... / Resting in our being's centre, we meet a world where everything in the same way rests in itself.

Then a tree becomes a mystery, the cloud a revelation, man a cosmos of whose riches we can only catch glimpses."

Hammarskjöld presents us with such glimpses in his haiku images and photographs. They are the fruits of the capacity to see, not in order to appropriate but to discover what a moment can offer, and then to test the ability to express it in words and pictures, to the satisfaction of the poet and the enjoyment of the reader.

HAIKU AND PHOTOGRAPHS

Slättnatt. En öde sal.
Kvinnan i fönsternischen
väntar solen.

Night on the plain. Deserted hall.
The woman in the window niche
awaits the sunrise.

This is a childhood memory from Uppsala. The first words show the Uppsala plain in the darkness of the night. Shows? One does not see the plain in the darkness but one imagines it and then one sees it dimly at dawn when the third line tells of the sunrise that is awaited.

From the plain the image jumps to a deserted hall. Here the perspective changes and the plain is seen not from the outside but from the inside of a hall. The images of plain and hall have close points of similarity and the adjective *deserted* enlarges the hall.

The poet has now introduced the stage of the action in the haiku and in the second line he introduces the actor:

The woman. It must be his mother, Agnes, who has been described as romantic and religious. Dag, the youngest child, was very close to her; the other three brothers were considerably older. The mother has gone out of the bedroom in the Uppsala Castle, where her husband Hjalmar resided as governor, and placed herself in the window niche to see the sunrise.

The first word of the Swedish text, *slättnatt,* is a combination of *slätt*, plain, and *natt*, night, and is an invention by Hammarskjöld, who often combines words into new contexts. This short word with four *t's* gives an assonance, a repetition of sounds, which is very effective—like a flourish of trumpets when the curtain opens.

Träden flämtar. Tystnad.
En droppe fårar tveksamt
rutans dunkel.

The trees pant. Silence.
A drop furrows hesitantly
the pane's dusk.

The first line presents a prospect which is not easy to
interpret. We see trees but we do not know which kind,
how many they are and in what light they stand. They are
depicted with sounds, nothing else. Pant means to breathe
heavily and fast. It must be the leaves which move quickly.
But we do not hear them in the wind, because the poet
asks for silence in the next word. The image gives rise to
foreboding.

The second line strengthens the apprehension. *A drop
furrows*—is it a tear? *Hesitantly* introduces slowness into
the image. We may see a tear slowly furrowing down a
wrinkled cheek, hesitant as to which wrinkle to choose.

If this is the image, our imagination has fooled us:
The third line shows that it is a raindrop furrowing a pane.
The dark apprehension of the image is here confirmed

by the information that the pane is dusky.

The perspective has changed. Having been outside we now move inside through the pane. From inside a room we see the slow movement of the raindrop on the pane. And beyond the pane we see the leaves of the trees quiver in the dusk.

The technique of describing a sensory impression with words from another sensory organ's impression, synaesthesia, occurs quite often in haiku, e.g. in Basho's (1644-1694) haiku "Stillness—/ into the rock pierces / the song of the cicadas." A sound cannot pierce a rock, but the visual image strengthens the impression of the shrilling sound of the cicadas.

Lyktskenets kon i diset.
Frostfjärilslek
kring den blanka stolpen.

The lamp's light cone in the haze.
Winter moths play
around the shiny post.

This is an elegant image of forms and light. The lamp's light forms a triangle with a circular basis against a hazy background. Into this cone of light flies a winter moth— or several—around the shiny post of the lamp. It is a geometrical painting with this long vertical line and a cone-formed centre of light which is broken through by circular movements.

The Swedish word *frostfjärilslek* (frost butterfly play) displays Hammarskjöld's skill of combining words into new words with new meaning. It is a very lyrical word which is difficult to render into other languages without losing the atmosphere.

In the beginning I thought that *frostfjäril* was a butterfly caught by autumn's first frost, but the encyclopaedia informed me that it is a name of a moth belonging to the family of geometrid moths which comprehends 15,000 species all over the world, of which 322 in Sweden. Most of them fly at night or at dusk—and perhaps searching for light as in Hammarskjöld's haiku.

Is winter moth a seasonal word? In Japanese haiku there is always a word indicating the season of the poem. William Higginson's *Haiku World*, an international poetry almanac, indicates *fuyu no cho*, winter moth in Japanese, as a seasonal word. The most typical image of a winter butterfly is *itecho,* freezing butterfly, which has left its cocoon on an unusually warm winter's day and sits with widespread wings to catch the heat of the sun.

Slätthorisonten
och murens lodstreck
korsas som ödeslinjer.

The plain horizon
and the wall's vertical
cross like fate lines.

Another haiku with geometrical lines, here a horizontal baseline of the plain's skyline, and the crossing vertical line of the wall. Hammarskjöld often describes lines in *Vägmärken* as an expression of his aesthetic sense but also with philosophical connotations.

Fate lines suggest the practice of telling fortunes by reading the lines on the palms of the hand, known as palmistry or chiromancy. The head line and the heart line lie across the palm and are crossed by the fate line from the wrist to the second finger.

Hammarskjöld often writes about destiny in *Vägmärken*, but the concept of fate lines is unusual. At Christmas time in 1956 he described his notes in the diary as "*Waymarks* set up when you reached a point where you needed them, a fixed point which must not be lost." These

notes were private, but since his life had changed he now reckoned with possible readers. "Perhaps you even desire them! Still, for someone it can be significant to see a way of destiny of which the man did not wish to speak while he was alive."

Pojke i skogen.
Kastande söndagsstassen
leker han naken.

> Boy in the forest.
> Throwing off his Sunday best
> he plays naked.

This is one of Hammarskjöld's most powerful haiku. The start is visual and fairy-like, perhaps evocative of Peter Pan, a boy alone among high trees.

The second line introduces a surprisingly dramatic action: the boy throws off his Sunday best. The reader imagines him neatly dressed by his mother in a Sunday outfit, then suddenly throwing it off in a rebellious action—and liberated, he plays naked.

There are photos of Dag as a child dressed in frocks. His mother had three sons and longed for a daughter. It was not unusual that mothers of the time dressed their little boys in frocks. This must have made them rebellious—like here Dag, who might have run out into the forest after attending a service at the Cathedral or after a long Sunday lunch. Finally he can start playing according to his own wishes. The image of the lonely naked boy among the trees also transmits a feeling of safety and security in the community of nature.

I slottets skugga
slöto sig blommorna
långt före aftonen.

In the castle's shadow
the flowers closed
long before evening.

His childhood's castle on the hill dominated the town. The rays of sunshine at dawn first hit Uppsala Castle before reaching the roofs of the town houses, and at the setting of the sun the largeshadow of the castle covered the garden long before nightfall.

The castle's shadow may also be interpreted as a symbol of his father's shadow over the son. Hjalmar Hammarskjöld was 43 years old when Dag was born, and the youngest son always felt a great distance between himself and his domineering father. Even Dag Hammarskjöld's tombstone lies in the shadow of his father's family monument in the Uppsala cemetery.

Mer än åren skilde dem
denna kvällstur
i den öde allén.

> More than years separated them
> on their evening round
> in the deserted alley.

Here the distance between father and son is painfully evident. The word *deserted* emphasizes the desolation in the image, further darkened by the dusk of the evening round. Father and son areframed by an alley with trees standing in line as uniformed sentries on their silent walk.

Dag Hammarskjöld had great respect for his father's sense of duty to serve the nation and international law, but at the same time he was in permanent conflict with this patriarch, whose "pressure I hated", as he said in a letter to his friend the painter Bo Beskow.

Örfilen lärde pojken
att hans faders namn
var dem förhatligt.

> The box on the ear taught the boy
> that his father's name
> was hateful to them.

This painful memory tells the story of his father's unpopularity after the war years 1914-1917, when as prime minister he governed Sweden and followed an uncompromising policy of neutrality which led to shortages and earned him the nickname "Hungerskjöld" (Hungershield).

This image is very dramatic and the only haiku I have seen which includes a box on the ear. After this violent introduction, the reason for the act in explained in the word *hateful* which is congruous with the box on the ear.

The poem does not tell who administered the blow. It seems unlikely that a schoolmate would have done it as parents' political actions generally do not influence the behaviour of schoolmates, so it might have been a teacher.

Han föll i volten.
Alla kunde skratta
åt en som var så feg.

> He fell in the somersault.
> Everybody could laugh
> at such a coward.

Another painful school memory. Hammarskjöld was proficient in gymnastics, but here he was ridiculed for failing to execute a somersault because he was too circumspect. To be laughed at like this because of cowardice is a terrible blow for a boy—especially a proud boy like Hammarskjöld.

48

Skolan slutat. Gården tömts.
Dem han sökte
funnit nya vänner.

School was over. The yard empty.
Those he sought
had found new friends.

A variation of the content of last poem, but here the introduction is concrete with the image of the empty schoolyard. He had once again come to play with his schoolmates, but they had left the yard and played, he understands, somewhere else with other friends. The word *empty* indicates that the yard earlier had been filled with schoolchildren.

Han var ej önskad.
När han likväl kom
fick han blott se dem leka.

He was not wanted.
When he nonetheless came
he could but watch them play.

The boy who came to play was not welcome to play with
the others. Another image of rejection. It was not only
class difference and his father's reputation which separated
him from his schoolmates. It was also what a friend wrote
to him: "You have one great failing—you take everything
too seriously." Hammarskjöld admits in a letter that it
can be "a great failing if one loses the sunny sense of
humour towards others and towards oneself, if one looses
the divine happy-go-lucky."

This poem is more of a haiku verse than a real haiku.
The first line is abstract, the second line turns from the
abstract to a concrete image, which is rendered visible
first with the word *play*.

Paketet föll i modden
men hon log bort oron
efter fallet.

The parcel fell in the mud
but she smiled away worry
after the mishap.

This is an image of mother and son walking on a muddy road and suddenly the boy drops his mother's parcel into the mud. He is alarmed, but her tender smile erases his worry.

The poems about his mother have quite another tone than the ones about his father. Here one sees the capacity of haiku to render deep and important relations between people through a small-scale image of few words. Haiku is often criticised for its inability to describe feelings, but the three lines avoid the wordy and direct descriptions which characterize other poems. Instead haiku describes a situation which indirectly evokes the feelings of the actors—feelings which also should be experienced by the readers.

Vid syrenhäcken
fri från "plikterna",
återfann hon ungdomslandet.

> By the lilac hedge,
> free from "duties",
> she again found the land of youth.

An image of the influence of nature in freeing people from the duties of social life. Here it is not the boy throwing off his Sunday best but the mother who feels young again by the lilac hedge, where she forgets all the duties which burden her as the wife of the governor. The family often talked about the duties which accompanied their privileged position in society. The son remembers with delight the moment when his mother Agnes, nearly forty when he was born, met him as a young and free woman amongst the scent and the colours of the lilac hedge. In Sweden, lilac blooms in June with the strongest scent of the summer, often described as romantically over-powering.

Kaprifolium.
I den grå skymningen
vaknade han till sitt kön.

Caprifolium.
In the gray twilight
he awakened to his sex.

Since childhood Dag Hammarskjöld was deeply interested
in nature and animals and often brought home flowers,
herbs and insects in small boxes. He was an early admirer
of Linnaeus, "the shining Prince of the Summer Land", as
he called him in an address in 1957 when the "King of
Flowers" was honoured, 250 years after his birth. Like
Linnaeus, Hammarskjöld liked to know the name of
everything he saw in nature, the stranger the names the
more joyously he expressed them in his poems in
Vägmärken and in his articles in the magazine of the
Swedish Tourist Association. The names invite the reader

into suggestive worlds: *Ice ranunculus, monk's-hood, Trollius and Pyrola, Pinguicula alpinas flowers, Epilobium's tall flower stalks, Saxifraga's manifoldness* . . .

When in the southern province of Skåne he sees rich growths of sea holly, sand pink or the white sand lily, his "botanical interest is reawakened from the slumber of the everyday flora" of his home province. When in the northern province of Lapland he sees the rich variety of flora, he depicts a "close-up of the mountain life, abundant enough to attract our full attention and to bring us into contact with its pulsating life."

It is typical for Hammarskjöld's haiku—and for haiku in general—to depict a close-up, rich enough to render the whole of a landscape or an atmosphere.

Caprifolium. A single word introduces the reader to the image. The caprifolium is a plant of the family Caprifoliaceae, the honeysuckle or the woodbine. They have two-labiate yellow or red flowers which give off scent in the evening. In the fragrance of the flowers the pubertal boy awakened to his sex.

Denna stenålderskväll
stod kyrkspiran på slätten
som en fallos.

This stone age evening
the church spire on the plain
erect like a phallus.

An image with several dimensions. The first line refers to an age when the male was basically the same male as he is today with his primitive lust. In ancient times fertility cults set up stones as phallic symbols. Here it is the church spire on the Uppsala plain which inspires Hammarskjöld's image.

The evening darkens the plain, while the church spire becomes more accentuated. The image reveals a lust and a longing which the holy symbol of the church spire cannot reject—nor satisfy.

This is a deliberately shocking image which indicates how a Christian sexual inhibition still yields to an indomitable urge. Without doubt Hammarskjöld's most anti-puritan poem in *Vägmärken*.

The metaphor is clearly expressed by the word *like*

(*som*) which compares the church spire to a phallus. Metaphors are seldom used in haiku, because the word is meant to speak for itself and not be compared to anything else in order to be accentuated or transformed in significance. But here the words acquire such a strong effect of contrast that the metaphor is motivated to lend desired excitement to the image.

Svarta stjärnskott.
Svalornas gälla skrin
när de paras i rymden.

Black shooting stars.
The swallows' shrill cries
as they mate in the sky.

The stars shine clear in space and draw bright lines when falling, but here they are black at the moment of shooting. In fireworks there is also black smoke from the discharge.

Swallows mate while on the wing, uttering shrill cries which can be perceived as white lines in contrast to the flapping black wings.

Basho writes about "the white cries of the wild ducks." Also the swallows are perceived by Hammarskjöld metaphorically as shooting stars in space. The poet remembers how the sight of the swallows mating burned in the body and the mind of the young man.

Vinterskymningen grånar
bakom rutan.
Burfågelns bröst blöder.

Winter twilight grays
beyond the pane.
The caged bird's breast bleeds.

At the window in the castle the young man may stand looking through the pane at the darkening winter twilight. He is longing to fly away from the cage of the castle, where his breast is bleeding. Where he wants to fly to he does not know, only that he wants to get away from the cold gray twilight of the Uppsala plain, this approaching dusk which will soon enfold the old castle and the heart of the encaged young man in the long darkness of night. *Grays* and *bleeds* depict a colour contrast—the red blood is the romantic colour of love and sacrifice. The image may evoke associations to paintings by the Swedish artist Nils Dardel.

Slottsfönstren såg dem.
I gråblåst och snö
filmades Karl den Tolfte.

The castle windows saw them.
In gray wind and snow
Charles the Twelfth was filmed.

Charles XII (1682-1718) was king of Sweden already at the age of 15. Like Hammarskjöld he felt a prisoner of his castle and he wanted to ride away to discover and conquer the world. He invaded Russia, was finally defeated by Peter the Great at Poltava and fled to the Ottoman Empire, from where he ruled Sweden for five years. He returned to his native country and was killed while besieging a fortress in Norway.

Hammarskjöld makes another reference to Charles XII in his *Waymarks*. In 1951, when Hammarskjöld was sworn in as a minister of the Swedish government in the presence of the king, he wrote about king Charles' coronation: "The immodesty of great pride: it lifts the crown from the cushion and places it upon the brow with its own hands." The young king set the crown on his own head, because he believed that he was appointed king by the grace of God. Hammarskjöld writes: "A fable to relate: about the crown that was so heavy it could be borne only by the one who was able to live in complete forgetfulness of its splendour." In many entries Hammarskjöld writes about the importance of acting and living in oblivion of the splendour of his position.

The first line of the haiku is interesting, because the castle windows are the spectators of the filming—not Hammarskjöld himself looking through the windows. The poet depersonalizes himself, which often comes about in haiku.

Han sänkte blicken
för att ej se kroppen
till att begära den.

He lowered his eyes
so as not to see the body
to desire it.

After the first line the reader wonders why he lowered his eyes, and in the second line we see what his eyes saw: a body. The third line gives the explanation: he wants to prevent desiring the body.

Dag Hammarskjöld admits in a note in *Vägmärken* (1952) that he was "shy about the nakedness of my own being" and that "without blinding desire, without feeling the right to intrude in another's life", he had difficulty in attaining "the complete harmony" which he required for a life together.

Vägrad den sökta
ville han förtjäna
att själv bli den sökte.

Denied the sought one,
he longed to deserve
to be the one sought.

Here Hammarskjöld sought out a girl or a young woman, who repudiated him, which must have hurt his feelings to such a degree that he decided to become the one sought out.

There are different rumours about the identity of the woman in question, but it was probably a young woman at the university of Uppsala who was courted by Dag Hammarskjöld and his friend Sven Stolpe, a promising young writer. Her name was Karin von Euler-Chelpin and she was a serious person with intellectual interests.

Several years ago I had the opportunity to ask Sven Stolpe about the truth of this rumour and he admitted that Dag courted Karin as well, "but I had a stronger will, so I married her." He has written in his memoirs that Dag "nobly stepped back."

Recently I asked Staffan Stolpe, son of Sven and Karin, about this episode, and he told me that his mother always had Hammarskjöld's photograph on her writing desk, even before he was appointed Secretary-General. She once told Staffan that she, regretfully, had not fully understood the seriousness of Dag's attentions.

Hemmet sände mig
till öde rymder.
Få söker mig. Få hör mig.

My home sent me
to deserted spaces.
Few seek me. Few hear me.

This is a remarkable poem from many aspects. Between my home and spaces there are wide distances in expanse, time and feeling. When one knows who the poet is, one understands the purport of his experience of being elevated to the leadership of the world organization.

It is more difficult to understand the meaning of the last line. How could this sought-out man, always surrounded by people, feel that few seek him and few hear him? The words *deserted spaces* evoke a feeling of loneliness. It must mean that the ones who he wants to seek him out and listen to him don't do it.

The words *deserted spaces* lead my thoughts to Saint-John Perse, whose great poem "Chronique" was translated into Swedish by Hammarskjöld, "Krönika." In *Vägmärken* there are several more or less hidden references to Perse's motifs and language, for instance the following:

> "The flutes of exile." Always among strangers to that
> which has formed you—*alone*.
> Always thirsting for the water from the springs—
> *captive*, not free to seek them.   (1957)

As a leading French diplomat, Alexis Léger (Saint-John Perse) fled from the German invasion of France and took refuge in the United States. There he wrote about "the flutes of exile", which continuously followed him.

There are close points of similarity between his estrangement and Hammarskjöld's sense of "deserted spaces." Perse writes about "deserted places, where the thirst for greatness rests." Hammarskjöld's *few hear me* evokes Perse's words about "the Princes of exile, and they have no need of my song." Not until after the war were Perse's poems from exile published in France. Among strangers in the "Land of Sunset" the French language became his real home.

Also for Hammarskjöld his native language became his home among those who were strangers to what had formed him. Few understood the depth and purity of his Swedish language which only *Vägmärken* was earmarked to receive.

He was always thirsting for the water from the springs, which means not only yearning for his language but also for the spiritual spring which he needed as a life-giving force in order to be able to execute the responsible work that had commandeered all his creative energies and so made him unfree. *The Stranger* in Perse's poem receives fresh water: "I predict for you a time of great joy and the bliss of the sources in our dreams."

In another entry of the same year (1957) Hammarskjöld quotes Saint-John Perse without indicating the source: "Il n'est d'histoire que de l'âme, il n'est d'aisance que de l'âme." *(There is no history but that of the soul, there is no peace but that of the soul)*

In this perspective *My home* in the haiku acquires a new meaning: What sent him to deserted spaces was not only the home of his childhood that had formed him but also "something from beyond which fills my being with the possibility of its origin." (1951) With Perse the flutes of exile are "the pure origin of our dreams."

Hammarskjöld's *something from beyond* has many names, among others *Slinger*, which is also used by Perse. With Hammarskjöld: "Once you grasped me, Slinger. Now into your storm. Now towards your goal." (1957)

Another name is "the One", which ends the entry in *Vägmärken* about "The flutes of exile": "The answer—the hard, clean, heavy answer: in the One you are never alone, in the One you are always at home." (1957)

73

Du återvänder aldrig.
En annan man
finner en annan stad.

You never return.
Another man
finds another city.

Haiku is about transformations. This haiku is about the transformation of a man and a city. They can never find each other as they once were.

The poem was composed after a visit Hammarskjöld paid to Uppsala in the summer of 1959. He was 54 years old and had been Secretary-General for six years. He looked at the city with other eyes than those of the child and the student. Memories arose and the mature man wanted to formulate them from his new perspective. It might have been at this moment that he decided to use haiku as the preferred form for his "memories."

This poem is philosophical with regard to content and general with regard to character. It does not provide any concrete image. Even if you know that the city refers to Uppsala, it is not possible to imagine the whole of the city, and especially, you cannot see the difference between what the city looked like in Hammarskjöld's memory and how it looked in the summer of 1959. Thus, the poem is not a true haiku but rather an epigram or an aphorism of seventeen syllables, that is to say, formed as a haiku verse.

This does not prevent the poem from transferring emotions, above all a feeling of melancholy that the poet seems to have experienced: Here I walked around, here I had all those strong feelings of friendship and loneliness, of my father's authority, of my mother's worries about her duties, of her forgiving smile...And then the self-controlled feeling of a matter-of-fact conclusion that it is never possible to return to the past.

Nordsångarens första drill.
Över bleka isar
tinar rymden.

> The northern warbler's first trill.
> Over pale ice fields
> space is thawing.

This is a haiku under the heading of "Summers", which comprehends 16 poems. They mostly deal with summer's flowers and trees, but this poem describes an experience of a migratory bird's first trill in early summer in Lapland. The northern warbler spends winters in Southeast Asia and summers in northern Europe, Asia and Alaska. When it comes to Sweden ice still covers the lakes but its colour is pale as it is thawing in the shining rays of the sun. Hammarskjöld used to walk in the mountains in June, first with his father, later with friends.

The haiku describes nature's transformation from winter to summer. Images of seasons' transformations are well-known in Japanese haiku. The slight shifts of colours indicate the changes in nature, here the pale colour of the ice thawing.

The poem starts with a quick vibrating sound from the sky. From the sky the eye turns to the ice fields and then back to space. These quick changes between movement and stillness, between detail and wide views constitute the strong points of this beautiful description of Swedish nature.

Myggdans. Masugnsrök.
Huggormen sov på stigen
till smultronstället.

Mosquito dance. Blastfurnace smoke.
Viper asleep on the path
to the wild strawberry patch.

Four different images in one haiku is unusual. Often two images are connected in a surprising way, like here the viper and the wild strawberry patch. It is difficult to give life and coherence to a poem that has three or four images.

It is also unusual to insert a full stop in the middle of a line. Here two different images in the first line are separated by a full stop, but they are connected by the moving cloud-formation of the mosquitoes and the blastfurnace smoke.

From these images there is quite a jump in the line of thought to the viper on the path. The viper guards the wild strawberry patch. This is the central image that Hammarskjöld wishes to convey. The dangerous reptile preventing him from reaching the sweet berries he was longing for. The situation recalls the dragon guarding the maiden. The hero has to pluck up courage in order to reach the goal. The wild strawberry patch may also be interpreted as paradise with the viper as the dangerous intruder.

As this exciting image with the viper captures the reader, he forgets the two images of the first line. They are left out, because they stand out as inessential and unnecessary in the context. It is most likely that Hammarskjöld inserted them in order to meet the requirement of 17 syllables. This haiku is an object-lesson in the conflict between the need for clarity and the perceived need to count syllables. It is better to lose some syllables in haiku than to add unnecessary elements to the image for mathematical reasons.

This haiku also demonstrates another difficulty that every haiku poet recognizes. He or she wants to include as much as possible of their experience in order to give a full picture of the situation. It is strenuous to erase facts and circumstances which were important to the poet at the time of the occurence, but in true haiku the writer must get used to leaving out superfluous matters.

The two first words in the Swedish original show Hammarskjöld's ingenuity at combining words into neologisms, typically compound nouns. This is possible in Swedish but impossible in most other languages. Therefore Swedish is very suitable for haiku.

Vid blixtnedslagen
trädde bruksherrarna
ned ur porträttens skuggland.

When lightning struck
the ironmasters stepped down
from their portraits' shadowland.

This is a sharply illuminated haiku with a surprise at the end. When the ironmasters appear in the second line, they are alive in the reader's mind. Then you see they are portraits on a wall. But in the sudden light of the lightning they come to life.

The compound noun *skuggland* (shadowland) is well-chosen as it contains several meanings. The portraits hang in a dark room or a dark corridor. The portraits may also be in dark colours, as was usual at the time. Portraits can also be seen as shadows of living people. The ironmasters are long since gone and thus resting in the shadowland of the dead.

This haiku image could be an image from an Ingmar Bergman film. The scared and watchful boy in "Tystnaden" (The Silence) walking through dark corridors in the old hotel in the alien city, or the timorous boy in "Fanny and Alexander" walking through secretive and ghostlike rooms in the winter night.

Branta svenska backar.
Framför kusken
ryckte hästländen svettig.

> Steep Swedish hills.
> In front of the coachman
> the sweaty twitch of the horse's loins.

This haiku also presents a scene that could have been taken from a film. The first line introduces a wide view of a landscape with steep hills. Then we see a coachman and in front of him we imagine reins in his hands. A further close-up shows the horse's loins, twitching and sweaty from the effort of pulling the carriage up the hills.

This poem demonstrates the importance of changing perspectives in haiku. The technical movement from the landscape to the coachman and then to the horse creates strong motion in the images which reinforces the movement of the content in the poem, the horse pulling the carriage. The perspective is that of the boy—he sits next to the coachman on the box and observes the twisting of the sweaty loins. This close-up transmits an impression of admiration for the power of the horse as well as compassion for the effort.

Vallfartsårens österland
vid den mörka ån
under lindarna.

Orient of pilgrimage years
by the dark stream
under the lindens.

Hammarskjöld alludes to a collection of poems by the Swedish writer Verner von Heidenstam entitled *Vallfart och vandringsår* (*Pilgrimage and years of wandering*, 1888). The first section of the book deals with memories and myths from the Orient.

This haiku presents a strong contrast between the colourful images of the Orient and the dark stream under the lindens (lime trees), where the young Hammarskjöld lies, reading about far away places. This is a romantic poem in the style of Shelley and Byron, expressing a sensual longing for another life.

Solflimrande
når flöjttonen gudarna
i födelsens grotta.

Sun-flickering
the flute notes reach the gods
in the cave of birth.

This poem starts a new chapter in Hammarskjöld's haiku writing with memories from "Fjärran" (Far away). It is an enchanting and mysterious image, mixed and dazzling by light and sound.

The notes of the flute are described as sun-flickering with their varying light and dark points. When the sensations of sight and hearing unite or change places, logic ceases and poetry takes over.

Hammarskjöld's haiku image has an Asiatic touch but is difficult to understand without any explanation. During a visit to Nepal in March 1959 he visited the great Buddhist

temple of Swayambhunat on a hill outside Kathmandu. He described his experience in an article in *National Geographic Magazine*: "Then we walked the narrow, circular road up the steep hill on the top of which the stupa dreamed its dream of a world beyond pain and vicissitude in the shadow of the timeless mountains . . . We were not far from the birthplace of the Buddha."

This place is Kapilavastu, now called Lumbini, situated at the foot of the Himalayas in the frontier territory of India. Stupa means crest and is a cone shaped mound or tower serving as a Buddhist shrine, often as a chamber of relics. Into the deep cave of birth, which for Hammarskjöld symbolizes the possibility of all origin, penetrate the notes of the flute with its message of life's rebirth.

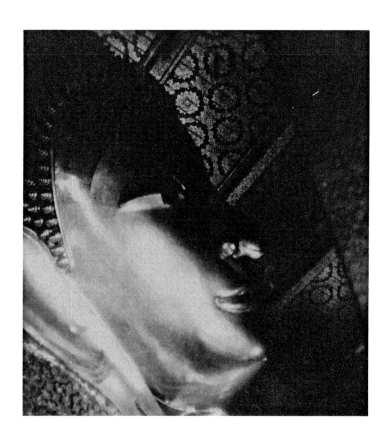

Himalayas isbranter
bortom kullarna
i påskens Vézelay.

       Himalaya's ice cliffs
       beyond the hills
       of Easter's Vézelay.

Also this experience is rendered in the article: "The air had the freshness of a spring night at Easter time in Burgundy. The association may seem farfetched, but the hills around led my thoughts to the land about Vézelay, where a shrine rises in the same way as a goal of pilgrimage."

The shrine is the historic basilica of St. Mary Magdalene, which Hammarskjöld discovered in 1948, when he was head of the Swedish delegation in Paris at the Marshall Plan negotiations on the reconstruction of Europe. His collaborators and family members have mentioned his interest in this basilica, among others his nephew Knut Hammarskjöld: "One Sunday Dag wanted to show me a discovery he had made some 140 miles southeast of Paris: We saw an accumulation of houses, a village with a church on the top of a hill. This, he explained, was Vézelay, and from here Richard Lionheart and Bernard de Clairvaux started the second crusade to Jerusalem. Dag was very fond of his discovery and during our walk in the narrow alleys he said that here he wanted to have a house in the shadow of the church for meditation and writing." (Essay in the book *Ringar efter orden* (*Rings from the words*), published 2005.)

Hammarskjöld never found a house in Vézelay but returned many times to the basilica, which also for him became a place of pilgrimage.

Apor. Månen väckt dem—
Kring världsnaveln
vredos stegens bönkvarnar.

Apes. The moon woke them—
Round the world's navel
turned the steps' prayer wheels.

Walking the narrow road up the steep hill to the shrine of Swayambhunat, "the stillness was broken by chattering screams and noises, and soon we were surrounded by monkeys, surprised but seemingly also pleased to get this unexpected company at a late hour."

In this sentence Hammarskjöld applies a typical haiku technique. When the reader hears the chattering screams and noises, his thought is led to human beings. Then it is disclosed that the cries came from apes. The thought is surprised and changes direction, creating some kind of haiku experience. Probably Hammarskjöld never thought that he heard the voices of men and women, but perhaps he did not understand the origin of the sounds. He was surely surprised by the sight of the apes, and has transmitted this surprise to the reader.

In his haiku he prefers to present the apes as a surprising introduction to the poem with only one word, which is most unusual in haiku. Here it is effective, because the image is unexpected and unexplained, which immediately arouses the imagination. After seeing the apes in our mind, we see the moon, another surprising sight. The explanation is that the moon woke the apes. It was probably Hammarskjöld and his group who woke the apes, but by pointing to the moon the poet informs us that it was dark and the moon was shining. This kind of indirect information is typical for haiku. Also for Buddhism, especially Zen, which enlightens man by satori, the sudden awakening. The full moon is a symbol of the awakening.

The concept of *the world's navel* returns the image of Buddha's birthplace, and *the steps' prayer wheels* is an elegant and concentrated image of monks walking around and around the stupa in the direction of the sun's movement while turning their prayer wheels. In his article Hammarskjöld writes: "The stupa rose against the night sky in a silence broken only by the light metallic sounds from the prayer wheels."* These images express the basic Buddhist ideas of an unending revolution of the universe and the cycle of time.

* Prayer wheel is a cylindrical box inscribed with or containing prayers, used especially by Buddhists of Tibet.

Rastplats. Koleldar tändas—
Sänkt i spegeldammen
vilar Vishnu.

Rest site. Charcoal fires are lit—
Submerged in the mirror pond
Vishnu rests.

This image of charcoal fires near a pond where the Hindu god of Vishnu is submerged, is suggestive and mysterious. Hammarskjöld illuminates the event in his article in the *National Geographic*: "Just outside the city (Kathmandu) lies a meadow surrounded by high trees but with a view across the valley to Swayambhunat. It is called the Twenty-two Fountains, for just where a steep hillside breaks the plain, there is a long stone ramp through which the cold waters of a mountain stream burst forth in many openings. It is a place steeped in the atmosphere of the mountains and yet stamped with the mark of ancient, high civilization, as sure in its artistic sense as in its sense of how to

create a harmonious interplay between the work of men and the surrounding landscape."

These sentences are highly visual and at the same time philosophical. After this concrete description of the cultural background Vishnu appears: "At the side of the ramp lies a small square pond built of stone, eroded by water and frost. Down into it lead worn steps. Resting in the pond lies a statue of the sleeping Vishnu, sunk so deep in the water that only the upper parts of the body break the surface. The moonlight played on the wet figure, contrasting with the red glow from fires burning a short distance from where we stood. The silence was of the kind that is to be found only in the mountains, a silence that is audible."

The charcoal fires were burning at a rest site and "round them were grouped pilgrims on their way to Swayambhunath, preparing their evening food without a word and without a glance at the strangers who passed." The pilgrims were Buddhist monks, and as a summary of this experience Hammarskjöld writes: "The sleeping Hindu god and the silent Buddhist monks crystallized two of the great spiritual currents that have grown out of the meeting between man and the mountains. They were of the mountains and of one spirit with the mountains. But they fused into the scenery the soul and the human perspective without which our feeling for nature is sterile and empty aestheticism."

These images are fascinating with their exotic content and sharp contours, at the same time they lift our thoughts to new knowledge and spiritual experiences. When Hammarskjöld expressed his observations in the form of haiku, he must have gone through the distress that every haiku poet feels from having to leave out so much of the experience. His haiku is focused on the essential: fire, water and Vishnu. By inventing the word *spegeldamm* (image pond) he may suggest that the fires are reflected in the water, but the tree lines left no space for the moonlight, nor for the sight of the upper parts of Vishnu's body breaking the surface.

In these four poems under the heading "Far away" Hammarskjöld has united three great religions in the same way as he united all the world's faiths in the block of iron ore illuminated by one shaft of light in the UN Meditation Room, an altar which is empty "only because it is dedicated to the God whom man worships under many names and in many forms."

Palmers sus och vågslag
blandades med psalmsången
från snölandet.

Sough of palms and beat of waves
blended with the hymns
from the land of snow.

In the winter of 1959-1960 Hammarskjöld undertook a
long journey through 25 countries and territories in Africa.
This haiku presents an image from a Swedish mission in
Guinea, West Africa, where he spent Christmas. Here,
as in the image of Himalaya and Vézelay, he combines
two geographical contrasts, the African beach with palm
trees and the Swedish land of snow.

The image is visually strong, but most interesting is
its use of sounds: soughs, wave beats, singing. The poet
hears the sounds of nature at the same time as he hears
and sings Christmas hymns. The sounds unite in a song
of praise.

Mässoffret i julnatten
bebådades dem
av trumpetstötar.

Christmas night mass—
the sacrifice announced to them
with trumpet fanfares.

The effect of this haiku also depends on sounds: mighty trumpet fanfares at Christmas night. The image leads our thoughts to angels blowing on trumpets to announce a divine message to man. On Christmas night the message is the birth of God's son. In Hammarskjöld's poem it is the Sacrifice of the Mass.

Sacrifice of the Mass is the Christian celebration of the Holy Communion interpreted as an act of sacrifice, when Christ's sacrifice on the cross is made present and invoked in prayers for the living and the dead.

The motif of sacrifice is a recurrent theme in *Vägmärken* ever since the first youthful notes. When they are linked together with the birth of Christ, as here, they connect to a thought noted in April 1953 after his election to Secretary-General: "That the way of calling ends on

the cross, the one who has accepted his destiny knows—
even when it has lead him through the jubilation around
Gennesareth or the triumphal entry into Jerusalem."

Kropparnas urladdning
i den varma nattens
flämtande åskljus.

The bodies' discharge
in the warm night's
flickering thunder light.

Just after the Christmas poems from West Africa follow
two haiku which express bodily discharge and desire. The
first poem is an explosion of the forces of man and nature
in a thundering light. The second poem is a sublimation
of desire in sun and tides:

Med en ilning av lust
sjönk kroppen soltung
i dyningens sälta.

With a thrill of desire
the body sank sun-drenched
in the tide's saltiness.

These poems about the lust-filled union of bodies and nature are mirrored in a note from 1951 in *Vägmärken*: "So rests the sky against the earth. In the tarn's dark stillness the forest's womb opens. And as the man enfolds the woman's body in his abiding tenderness, so the nakedness of the ground and the trees is enfolded in the morning's still, high light."

This scene of love's union echoes an aching expression of unfinished personal longing in the note that follows: "I myself feel an ache which is a longing for union, for participation, for sharing in this meeting. An ache which is identical with the desire of earthly love—but directed toward ground and water and sky, answered by the whispering of the trees, the fragrance of the soil, the caresses of the wind, the embrace of light and water. Satisfied? No, no, no. But refreshed, rested—while waiting."

Hammarskjöld's prose is filled with poetry and singing rhythms—like the last sentence in this tender sublimation.

Snö i april.
Kardinalen sökt skydd
i den vita Forsythian.

>Snow in April.
>The cardinal sought shelter
>in the white forsythia.

The first line paints a scene of something unusual: snow in April. The image is white even if it may suggest some buds in the spring.

In the second line the actor enters—the cardinal—who wears another colour, red.

In the third line, white returns, here covering the branches and the flowers of the forsythia.

Forsythia bearing yellow flowers is also called Golden Bell. In some species the yellow flowers appear before the leaves in early spring. The attribute *white* before *forsythia* would be surprising if the reader did not already know that it was snowing.

But still the image indicates a transformation as the inner eye lays a white colour over the yellow flowers. The surprise would have been even stronger if the first line's explication had been placed at the end of the haiku.

To a Swedish reader the image of the cardinal seeking shelter in the shrub is intriguing, as we generally presume that the cardinal is a priest in a red frock. The bird envisaged, common along America's northeastern coastline, is unknown in Sweden. Perhaps it amused Hammarskjöld that Swedish readers might be confused by this word of two meanings.

På salongsbordet
blev boken solkig
och gick texten förlorad.

On the parlor table
the book became soiled
and the text was lost.

A very concrete image with a philosophical content. *Salongsbordet* in Swedish refers to the table in the best room, where *the book became soiled*. Why, one wonders. From ashes of the fire-place? It seems improbable that the cover of a book honoured by a favoured place in a room visited by an important guest like Hammarskjöld was dusty.

In the third line the word *soiled* receives another meaning as information indicates that also the text was *lost*. The cover of the book was not soiled, but the whole book was impure in its environment. The text was lost to those who stayed or resided in the elegant room, as they did not read or understand the book. This valuable book was, according to the poet, in the wrong place and thus only an ornament.

The haiku mirrors Hammarskjöld's negative attitude to frivolous social life with cocktail party small talk. In his youthful letters and in his notes in *Vägmärken* he expresses disgust at babble and chatter which "degrades the living reality." He is disgusted at his own clown role which he plays in order to capture and at least for a while command the attention of a person "whose feelings he does not dare to test through revealing his own." (1950)

He accuses himself of weakness at moments when he prefers to entertain rather than being left alone. And when finally alone, tired of people, he often complains at being too tired to fill his solitude with something meaningful.

När gudar spelar
söker de en sträng
som ej rörts av människor.

> When the gods play
> they seek a string
> untouched by men.

One of the first entries in *Vägmärken* speaks of "the stretched strings of the soul" quivering as beauty flies by. Beauty is "the wind that refreshes the traveller." Already in his first entry he says: "Touched by the wind / from my unknown goal / the strings quiver / while waiting."

Thus, what touches the strings is the wind that the touched one feels but cannot see, nor can anyone else. The wind comes from his "untouched goal", perceived already in his youth but which he definitely acknowledges as God only at a mature age.

In order to make the goal visible the gods look for *a string untouched by men*, the haiku says. The prerequisite for usefulness is spiritual purity. Already in his sixth entry in the diary Hammmarskjölds declares that he must "dare to be himself." What he then can gain is that "the greatness

of life is reflected in you according to the measures of your purity."

This means that he in his depth recognizes a string of stillness which must remain pure for the gods, God, to play on so as to produce a "clear, simple note in the silence." A note which has "the liberating purity and revealing sharpness of the revelation", and which makes people listen.

The uncertainty of *while waiting* passes into certainty when he, after being called to his high post, recognizes that he is "consecrated—because my destiny is to be used and used up according to Your will." He has thus passed the test, answered "Yes to God: yes to his destiny and to yourself."

Guden tog mandom
i den offrade
när han valde att offras.

> God took the form of man
> in the offered one
> when he chose to be offered.

The previous poem had partly a visual image while this poem of the same genre expresses an idea without any concrete image, which makes it a poem of haiku form but not a real haiku.

The poem describes an incarnation, how God enters man and became man *when he chose to be offered.* The one alluded to is the historical Jesus but could also mean Hammarskjöld himself, making these lines a sequel to the previous poem.

Already in the second entry in *Vägmärken* Hammarskjöld speaks of sacrifice: a young man "ever ready to gather everything / into a single sacrifice." The translator W.H. Auden writes in his foreword to *Markings*, "I simply cannot believe that, at the age of twenty, Hammarskjöld thought in exactly the same terms as he was to think in thirty years later." Auden assumes that Hammarskjöld did not write this entry and other entries of the same kind at the time but added them later.

The Swedish copyright holders protested against this allegation and asked Auden to delete these "unfounded fantasies" from the foreword, but Auden did not change anything.

The discovery of Hammarskjöld's letters to his young friends in Uppsala of the 1920s prove that Hammarskjöld did indeed think that way at the time. In a letter from 1928 to Jan Waldenström he describes sacrifice through death as the final offering to life. The letter is interesting because it offers a clear definition of sacrifice: It is "a sacrifice of everything exterior for the perfection of the interior and for the fulfilment of the undertaking."

Hammarskjöld was in this respect obviously influenced by his mother's strong religious belief in serving God and his father's traditional belief in serving the nation, selflessly disregarding personal concerns.

The years pass and Hammarskjöld prays for "something to live for, great enough to die for." (1952, the year before the UN nomination)

Ensam i sin dolda växt
fann han gemenskap
med allt växande.

Alone in his hidden growth
he found fellowship
with all growing things.

Alone—because while he was alive he did not want to speak
about the way of destiny to which he had dedicated his
life—thus *hidden. Growth*: With his "yes to his destiny"
he grew as a man—not only I, "but God in me."

In his loneliness among people he found *fellowship
with all growing things*. This may be interpreted as a
pantheistic union of everything that grows and develops
in nature, including a sensual union with earth, sea,
winds—already mentioned—but it also means a
fellowship with all spiritual growth, from the writings of
the mystics to poetry, music and the arts.

Hammarskjöld was inspired by the ideas for creative development of Henri Bergson, the French philosopher. The driving force of all growth and development is, according to Bergson, an interior creative life force, which makes possible new forms of life and explains the leaps in creation. Life is essentially freedom and expresses itself in its first manifestations of primitive organisms as an aptitude for change.

Henri Bergson was well known in Sweden since he received the Nobel Prize for Literature in 1927. He influenced the writings of Nathan Söderblom, Archbishop of Uppsala and a close friend of the Hammarskjöld family. Dag Hammarskjöld based several of his UN speeches on the evolution theories of Bergson, above all that reality is essentially spiritual and that all time is borne by the past, the breeding ground of all growth.

Detta tillfälliga
möte av möjligheter
kallar sig Jag.

> This accidental
> meeting of possibilities
> calls itself I.

This intellectual poem with seventeen syllables is far away from the concrete reality of haiku. It is also far away from Hammarskjöld's deterministic view of destiny. It reflects Henri Bergson's view of development as a chain of accidental choices. This view has been confirmed by science in its discovery that only one of millions of sperms reaches the egg to fertilize it. To call himself *Jag* (I) with a capital letter seems to Hammarskjöld presumptuous as millions of other *jag* (I) could have been procreated from the same meeting.

In an entry from 1951 in *Vägmärken* he writes about a flash of insight: "*You could just as well never have existed.* With regular salary, a bankbook, and a briefcase under your arm, it is presupposed that you take yourself for granted. What you are can be of interest, not that you are. The pension—not death—is what you should think about 'as long as the day lasts' ".*

This entry is full of irony and existential meditation. Like everybody else Hammarskjöld has adapted himself to his career and is real in relation to other people because he has a position, not because he exists as a human being. This life ends with a pension, while the mystery of death does not preoccupy people. The great questions which Hammarskjöld finds of value to ponder upon seem to be without importance to other people.

* Refers to John 9:4: "As long as the day lasts / I must carry out the work of the one who sent me."

Träden, vattnen, månskäran—
allt denna kväll
i skälvande osmos.

Trees, waters, crescent moon—
all this night
in trembling osmosis.

Osmosis describes the tendency of fluid substances, if separated by a permeable or porous membrane, to filter through it and become equally diffused. The separation of trees, waters and the crescent moon filter through the night and are united in trembling interaction. Visually, the background of this image is perhaps the reflection of trees and moon on the rippled surface of the water.

Hammarskjöld often lifts his concrete observations to an abstract philosophical or spiritual level in order to find a unifying formula for existence. His key word is *integrity,* which means not only absolute honesty between mind and action but also the combination of all parts into a whole.

Risk och renhet—
i denna kamp mot fjället
med mig själv som motstånd.

> Risk and purity—
> in this struggle with the mountain
> with myself as resistance.

In the middle of this abstract poem there is a concrete image of the poet himself in the mountain. It is described as a struggle with the mountain, which leads thoughts to the mountain climber struggling to ascend a precipice. But in the third line appears the surprising information that it is not the mountain that offers resistance but himself.

The struggle with the mountain is in reality a struggle with his own comfort, laziness, weakness, the temptation to give in before reaching your goal. If you give in to this resistance you never obtain the satisfaction of victory, but

experience the lack of determination as treachery.

However, in this struggle there is an experience that Hammarskjöld formulated already in his early twenties: "Never measure the mountain's height until you have reached the top. Then you will see how low it was." Forward! Forward! he exclaims thirty years later (1956): "Whatever the distance that I have put behind me, it does not give me the right to stop." Every new height arouses enticement and resistance.

In the struggle there is always a *risk* of failing and falling, but risk is part of all challenge, and without risk there would be no joyous feeling of victory and triumph.

Purity is an experience that Hammarskjöld always denotes in connection with mountains, where silence and vast expanses provide the mind and the senses with a space that liberates the earthbound and social self. Here he can reach "the extra-human in the experience of the greatness of nature." (1951)

This perspective is the utmost in the poem: to surmount the adherence to the human self in order to attain union with the extra-human.

Hammarskjöld was often described as a "mountain romantic" or "alpine romantic", but such an epithet limits him, as his thoughts on high altitudes generally soar to even higher philosophical and spiritual heights. In his article about the Himalayas in *National Geographic*

Magazine he writes: "To someone who has learned to love the mountains and see in mountaineering one of the most satisfactory ways we can test our ability against nature—yet basically as a tribute to nature—it is somewhat shameful to approach the Himalayas by plane. My last words here should be a tribute to our pilot, who did his job with a deep insight and love of the mountains that characterize the true mountaineer. He managed to convey, at least to this passenger, a bit of the feeling of liberty, strength, and harmony we achieve when we fight the mountain and live with it, helped only by our body and our mind."

Once again, the idea that the struggle with nature is a tribute to nature, which tests the intrinsic value of man—that is, his purity and moral strength. And in the following sentence he soars even higher: "The contrast between the sovereign quiet of the mountaintop and the wild ranges leading in toward it added to the otherworldliness, the feeling that we had penetrated into a world of cosmic purpose and character."

Ännu långt från stranden
lekte havets friskhet
i bronsblanka löv.

Still far from the shore
the freshness of the sea played
in bright bronze leaves.

A reflection on nature which has a strong resemblance to Hammarskjöld's photos with their long lines and sweeping views ending in a close-up of leaves.

In the first line you see a long shore, even if far away.

In the second line the view changes to the sea and its waves playing in the sun.

In the third line you are surprisingly brought back to land and to trees with shiny leaves.

The wind from the sea has brought the freshness of the sea to leaves far away from the shore. Together with the wind the reader has made a long journey across shore and sea and land.

The word *lekte* (*played*) indicates that the image is a memory. If the poet had used the present tense, the image would have been prolonged.

Denna morgon
fyllde fågelsången sinnet
med nattens svala ro.

> This morning
> the singing of birds filled the mind
> with the night's cool stillness.

This haiku needs no comment. It speaks for itself, as many haiku do.

Risking intervention, however, I would like to single out the soft transition from night to morning, revealed by the singing of birds. When the birds are heard in the morning, it usually means an awakening to light and activity, but here the singing leads to a prolongation of the night. It is a musical transition from a long silence. But behind the words you have a feeling of disquietude, cooled by the night's rest and blown away this morning by the birds' singing.

När den ej fann en maka
kallade man
enhörningen pervers.

When it did not find a mate
they called
the unicorn perverted.

This poem is about myths. Hammarskjöld was very fond of the unicorn image, an animal nobody had seen but many had painted. Nor had anyone seen Hammarskjöld's inner life as it had been drawn in *Vägmärken*, his "only true 'profile'", visible first after his death. On his desk he kept a small silver unicorn mounted on a piece of black wood, which Bill Ranallo, his personal aide/bodyguard, once gave him for his birthday. After Ranallo's death with Hammarskjöld in the air crash, Mrs. Ranallo kept the unicorn.

Hammarskjöld was certainly conscious of the Oriental origin of the unicorn. One of the oldest mythical tales in India is about a gazelle hind drinking water in a river next to the hut of a hermit, whose sperm she happens to swallow, and thus Rsyasrnga, also called Unicorn, is born. This gazelle is a holy animal which is seduced by a princess in a country hit by drought. Their love makes the rain fall and the earth become green again. The horn is a symbol of fertility but also described as an image of the moon on the wane which announces the arrival of the monsoon.

The legend of the unicorn travelled eastwards to China (*chi'lin*) and Japan (*kirin*), and westwards to the Middle East and Europe. In China the unicorn emerged from the Yellow River with the first Chinese characters on its back, and this writing was later brought to Japan.

In the Christian world the unicorn symbolized Christ's incarnation as well as the chivalrous lover. The unicorn could be captured only by setting out a chaste maiden in the forest. Enticed by her purity the unicorn came to her, resting in her lap and falling asleep. Then the hunters could pounce.

Hammarskjöld was probably amused by the universal divine symbolism of the unicorn, especially as this holy animal was generally painted with blue eyes.

If Hammarskjöld was ever seduced by a chaste maiden, nobody alive would probably know, but he certainly described his attraction to women in several entries in

Vägmärken. He writes about the "aching beauty" of a neckline, and in a letter, of a woman with "the most beautiful eyes I ever saw."

The word myth has also come to imply a false notion widely disseminated, to which Hammarskjöld refers when writing that the unicorn was called perverted when it did not find a mate. Brian Urquhart gives the following explanation in his great biography of *Hammarskjöld* (1972, page 27): "Stupid or malicious people sometimes made the vulgar assumption that, being unmarried, he must be a homosexual, although no one who knew him well or worked closely with him thought so. When he was confronted, in the first month of his Secretary-Generalship, with the rumours to this effect then being put about by his predecessor, Hammarskjöld remarked that if there had been any element of truth in the story, he would not, and could not in the prevalent state of public opinion on the question of homosexuality, have accepted the office. The homosexual rumour was resurrected from time to time by various detractors when he was under political attack."

The predecessor was Trygve Lie, a Norwegian who detested the idea that his successor was a Swede, especially as Hammarskjöld's nomination had been proposed by the French and the British UN ambassadors, who had asked Lie to resign from his office in advance, because the work of the UN was paralysed since the Soviet Union refused to co-operate with Lie whom they regarded as too pro-American.

Skapar du? Förintar du?
Detta är frågorna
för din järnbörd.

           Do you create? Do you destroy?
           These are the questions
           for your ordeal-by-fire.

The word *järnbörd* means holding a piece of glowing iron or walking on glowing iron in order to establish one's innocence. Hammarskjöld himself was to die in a sea of fire, but he was thrown away from the wreck of the crashed airplane and was the only victim not burned.

This poem, where only *järnbörd* (ordeal-by-fire) depicts something concrete, was written in the autumn of 1959 and thus one year before the beginning of the Congo crisis and two years before his death at Ndola in Africa on the night between 17 and 18 September. The Congo crisis brought despair to him when the UN troops, "the soldiers of peace", became involved in armed battles, against the Secretary-General's instructions and his personal intentions. In free verses of 1961 he expressed his anguish already noted in the haiku:

Late night hours'
sleepless questions:
Did I act correctly?
and why did I act
as I did?

He feels "naked against the target", "arrows whistle" at
him—and still:

What do I fear?
If they strike
and kill,
what is this
to bewail?

Others have gone before.
others will follow—

Medan skotten ekade
sökte han ordens liv
för livets skull.

While the shots echoed
he sought the life of words
for life's sake.

The Secretary-General sought the right words to activate the process of peace negotiations in the midst of armed hostilities. Generally speaking, the words already exist in the Charter of the United Nations, which all member states have promised to respect and obey, but when its principles are not followed, the Secretary-General must intervene to give life to the words so that they will be experienced as real by the parties that have gone back on their words. The reason for giving life to the words is to save lives, that is, a duty to intervene *for life's sake.*

Hammarskjöld's respect for words and their use with

the strictest care and in uncompromising love of truth was well known and certified. He stated in *Vägmärken* that "respect for the word is the first requirement in the discipline through which man can be educated to maturity—intellectually, emotionally and morally." This respect was also a condition for the growth of society and the human race. (1955)

The poem can also be interpreted as love of language, a necessity for Hammarskjöld to practice even *while the shots echoed*. And perhaps especially at such times in order to find life in words and thus counteract the death that men wreak with their weapons.

It is hard to avoid thinking of this poem when one sees Hammarskjöld in the plane over the Congo on his last journey to mediate peace between the central government in Leopoldville and the seceding province of Katanga, while he translates Martin Buber's philosophical work *Ich und Du* from German to Swedish. In his briefcase among the parts of the wrecked plane was the UN Charter, the Bible in English, St. James version, Buber's work and Hammarskjöld's notebook with translated texts: "It is our destiny's high, painful melancholy that every You in our world will be an It. /. . . / And not even love can remain in an immediate relation: it subsists but changing between actuality and potentiality."

In an interview in the French magazine *Figaro Littéraire* (5.11.1960) Hammarskjöld says that he devotes at least two hours a day to *"choses sérieuses",* serious things, that is literature. This shows his priorities.

Arsareths morgonljus
långa vårkvällar
som sökte sin mening.

> Arsareth's morning light
> long spring evenings
> which sought their meaning.

Arsareth is a Hebrew name that means "another land." It is interesting to note that the first and the last entry in *Vägmärken* describe "an unknown land." In the first entry of 1925, when Hammarskjöld was 20 years old, he wrote:

> I am being driven farther
> into an unknown land.
> The ground becomes harder,
> the air more incitingly cold.
> Moved by the wind
> from my unknown goal
> the strings quiver
> while waiting.

> Still questioning
> shall I arrive,
> where life rings out—
> one clear simple note
> in the silence.

The strings quiver while the young man is waiting, but not before the end of his path will they ring out with a clear and simple tone.

The last entry, dated 24 August 1961, twenty-four days before his death, starts with the following words:

> Is it a new land
> in another reality
> than day's?
> Or have I lived there,
> before the day?

After a description of dream images of a mountain landscape in different seasons, the poem ends with the following words:

> But it is the same land.
> And I begin to know the map
> and the points of the compass.

Against this background the meaning of the haiku becomes clearer. The Bible passage of 2 Esdras 13:45 explains the vision of the coming of Messiah: "Through that region there was a long way to go, a journey of a year and a half; and that country is called Arzareth." It is said that ten tribes were wondrously brought to this country, from whence they will return in the last times.

"And the Lord rooted them out of their land in anger, and in wrath, and in great indignation, and cast them into another land, as it is this day." (Deuteronomy 29:28)

Did the young Dag Hammarskjöld feel that he belonged to a tribe that was rooted out of their land and one day would return? Did he ponder about such questions in the long spring evenings when he pondered his meaning? The mature man then discovered that it is not a new land he was brought to, but the same land, even if it shows another reality.

För den som tror
skall det sista undret
bli större än det första.

For him who believes
the last miracle
shall be greater than the first.

This abstract poem is the last one in Hammarskjöld's haiku collection of 1959. His next entry is from Easter 1960 and is about forgiveness and sacrifice. This poem is about faith and miracle.

The *last miracle* must refer to the miracle that the believer is expected to meet at death. No one alive knows anything about this, but with Hammarskjöld's words this miracle shall be greater for the believer than the first one.

Which was the first one? The miracle to be born as a human being, to exist with consciousness? When he chose to be offered and "God took human form"? When did that happen? His answer in *Vägmärken*—noted Whitsunday 1961—is not exact: "I once did answer yes to someone—or something. From that time comes my certainty that existence is meaningful and that my life, therefore, in self-surrender, has a goal".

154

'SINGLE FORM'

Dyningen som faller	The breaking wave
muskeln när den spännes	the muscle as it stretches
lyder samma lag.	obey the same law.
Linjens lätta böjning	The line's light curve
samlar kroppens kraftspel	gathers the body's play of strength
i en djärv balans.	in a bold balance.
Skall mitt sinne finna	Shall my mind find
denna stränga kurva	this strict curve
på sin väg till form?	on its way to form?

This poem, from *Vägmärken* 1958, contains three verses, each with 17 syllables in three lines. Even if the two first verses also contain independent images, it is not possible to describe them as haiku, as they show observed phenomena rather than shaping surprising transformations. Hammarskjöld has, rightly, not included these verses among his haiku, as they comprehend a linked unit with parts dependent of each other. Furthermore the poem has a title, which is not customary in haiku, above all because the title reveals some of the content, thus weakening the element of surprise.

The title 'Single Form' is the name of the sculpture by Barbara Hepworth erected in 1964 in front of UN Headquarters in New York as a memorial to Dag Hammarskjöld. During his time she had made a wooden sculpture with the same name, much smaller than the present ten-foot high bronze sculpture. The poem is a tribute to an artist and a form of art which became very important to Hammarskjöld.

The first contact between Dag Hammarskjöld and Barbara Hepworth took place in 1956, when he was looking for a sculpture worthy of the paintings in his office by Picasso and Matisse on loan from the Museum of Modern Art. He chose a work by Hepworth, and on Christmas Day 1956 wrote to her: "It will give me a constant joy to have one of your works before my eyes."

This was the first letter in a correspondence that lasted until his death in September 1961. The words in Hammarskjöld's letters express great admiration for her artistry and her letters express the same admiration for his ethical work to create a world of peace and order. They met and their exchange of letters became more intimate and took the form of a restrained passion.

They had a similar outlook on beauty and ethics and found that they belonged to the same generation of fighting optimists who wanted to build a new world on the ruins of the one devastated materially and morally by two world wars.

They were also alike in shyness in their personal encounters. Immediately after a meeting Barbara Hepworth wrote and excused herself for being utterly inarticulate: "There was much that I wanted to say—& I said nothing; I do ask you to forgive me./. . . / I cannot thank you enough for those last minutes on Sunday evening—an unexpected moment of arrested time which you invested with a special grace—& which for me has become a charge which I hope to fulfil."

After a visit to her exhibition in London in June 1961 Hammarskjöld wrote: "It was a sunny moment, full of impressions of perfect beauty, but beauty used as a road to some fundamental experiences and, if I may say so, expressions of faith." The letter ended with a promise that "we shall, for our part, continue as well as we can to model in action and words what you are so fortunate to express, to perfection, visibly and tangibly."

We means the United Nations—or more exactly Hammarskjöld incarnating the world organization. *Shall my mind find this strict curve on its way to form?*

Hepworth expresses her gratitude that her work is seen through the eyes of somebody of Hammarskjöld's "immense integrity." Hammarskjöld writes that "your 'Single Form' stands as a sentinel, representing the integrity both of the artist and of this operation." He adds the following words: "My first impression (of your work) is one of great beauty but also of an increasing sense of the drama of the present fight between sub-human chaos and human creative order." The letter was written in October 1960 in the midst of the Congo operation and its political drama.

Hammarskjöld's last letter to Barbara Hepworth is dated 11 September 1961, the day before his departure from New York to the Congo. He refers to a new sculpture which she has sent him: "I have now had it before me a couple of weeks, living with it in all shades of light, both physically and mentally, and this is the report: it is a strong and exacting companion, but at the same time one of deep quiet and timeless perspective in inner space. You may react to the word exacting, but a work of great art sets its own standard of integrity and remains a continuous reminder of what should be achieved in everything." Six days later he was dead.

In Barbara Hepworth, Hammarskjöld found an exacting companion, who saw and responded to his passionate inner nature. At the unveiling of 'Single Form' in front of United Nations Headquarters on 11 June 1964 Barbara Hepworth said: "Dag Hammarskjöld had a pure and exact perception of aesthetic principles, as exact as it was over ethical and moral principles. I believe they were, to him, one and the same thing, and he asked of each one of us the best we could give."

Their exchange of letters testifies that Hammarskjöld also became united emotionally with the universal integrity that he, according to his apprehension, had already been united with intellectually, ethically and aesthetically.

The sculpture 'Single Form' has a narrowing base, which makes it rest lightly on the ground, and a circular hole close to the top which unites it with the surrounding space. Light on the ground and the hole uniting man with space. Or in Dag Hammarskjöld's own words in *Vägmärken*: "For every deed less and less bound to your name, for every step more lightly treading the earth" (1956), and "in the One you are never alone, in the One you are always at home." (1957)